LOOK FOR T
technique videos

M000013422

CELEB
Slouchy
BEANIES *for the family* Book 2

"Is that somebody famous?" That's what everyone will be wondering when they catch a glimpse of you wearing one of these slouchy beanies inspired by celebrity fashions. Designed by Lisa Gentry, here are caps to crochet for everyone in the family.

LEISURE ARTS, INC. • Little Rock, Arkansas

EASY +

Size: Small/Medium {Large/X-Large}

Fits Head Circumference: 20½{22½}"/52{57} cm

SHOPPING LIST

Yarn (Medium Weight)

[7 ounces, 370 yards
(198 grams, 338 meters)
per skein]:

☐ Navy - 1 skein

☐ Blue - 1 skein

Crochet Hook

☐ Size I (5.5 mm)

or size needed for gauge

Size Note: We have printed the instructions for the sizes in different colors to make it easier for you to find:

• Size Small/Medium in Blue

• Size Large/X-Large in Green

Instructions in Black apply to both sizes.

GAUGE INFORMATION

14 dc and 7 rnds = 4" (10 cm)

Gauge Swatch: 3" (7.5 cm) diameter
Work same as Body through Rnd 2: 24 dc.

——STITCH GUIDE——

SINGLE CROCHET 2 TOGETHER
(abbreviated sc2tog)

Pull up a loop in each of next 2 dc, YO and draw through all 3 loops on hook (**counts as one sc**).

INSTRUCTIONS
Body

With Navy, ch 5; join with slip st to form a ring.

Rnd 1 (Right side)**:** Ch 3 (**counts as first dc, now and throughout**), 11 dc in ring; join with slip st to first dc changing to Blue (*Fig. 3, page 46*); do **not** cut Navy: 12 dc.

Rnd 2: Ch 3, dc in same st as joining, 2 dc in next dc and in each dc around; join with slip st to first dc changing to Navy; do **not** cut Blue: 24 dc.

Rnd 3: Ch 3, dc in same st as joining, 2 dc in next dc and in each dc around; join with slip st to first dc changing to Blue: 48 dc.

Rnd 4: Ch 3, dc in next 4 dc, 2 dc in next dc, (dc in next 5 dc, 2 dc in next dc) around; join with slip st to first dc changing to Navy: 56 dc.

Rnd 5: Ch 3, dc in next 2 dc, 2 dc in next dc, (dc in next 3 dc, 2 dc in next dc) around; join with slip st to first dc changing to Blue: 70 dc.

Rnd 6: Ch 3, dc in next 5 dc, 2 dc in next dc, (dc in next 6 dc, 2 dc in next dc) around; join with slip st to first dc changing to Navy: 80 dc.

Size Small/Medium ONLY

Rnd 7: Ch 3, dc in next dc and in each dc around; join with slip st to first dc changing to Blue.

Rnd 8: Ch 3, dc in next dc and in each dc around; join with slip st to first dc changing to Navy.

Rnds 9-14: Repeat Rnds 7 and 8, 3 times; at end of Rnd 14, cut Blue.

Rnd 15: Ch 1, sc in same st as joining and in next 2 dc, sc2tog, (sc in next 3 dc, sc2tog) around; join with slip st to first sc, do **not** finish off: 64 sc.

Size Large/X-Large ONLY

Rnd 7: Ch 3, dc in next 6 dc, 2 dc in next dc, (dc in next 7 dc, 2 dc in next dc) around; join with slip st to first dc changing to Blue: 90 dc.

Rnd 8: Ch 3, dc in next dc and in each dc around; join with slip st to first dc changing to Navy.

Rnd 9: Ch 3, dc in next dc and in each dc around; join with slip st to first dc changing to Blue.

Rnds 10-16: Repeat Rnds 8 and 9, 3 times; then repeat Rnd 8 once **more**; at end of Rnd 16, cut Blue.

Rnd 17: Ch 1, sc in same st as joining and in next 2 dc, sc2tog, (sc in next 3 dc, sc2tog) around; join with slip st to first sc, do **not** finish off: 72 sc.

Band - Both Sizes

Rnds 1-5: Ch 1, sc in same st as joining and in each sc around; join with slip st to first sc.

Finish off.

ZIGZAG

▰▰▱▱ **EASY +**

SIZE INFORMATION

Size: Small {Medium-Large}

Fits Head Circumference: 19{21-23}"/48.5{53.5-58.5} cm

Yarn (Medium Weight)

MEDIUM
4

[7 ounces, 370 yards (198 grams, 338 meters) per skein]:

☐ Grey - 1 skein

☐ Black - 1 skein

Crochet Hook

☐ Size I (5.5 mm)

or size needed for gauge

Size Note: We have printed the instructions for the sizes in different colors to make it easier for you to find:

• Size Small in Blue

• Size Medium in Pink

• Size Large in Green

Instructions in Black apply to all sizes.

GAUGE INFORMATION

5 V-Sts and 9 rnds = 4" (10 cm)

Gauge Swatch: 3" (7.5 cm) diameter

Work same as Body through Rnd 2: 12 V-Sts.

——STITCH GUIDE——

V-ST (uses one st or sp)

(Sc, ch 1, dc) in st or sp indicated.

INSTRUCTIONS
Body

With Grey, ch 5; join with slip st to form a ring.

Rnd 1 (Right side)**:** Ch 3 **(counts as first dc)**, 11 dc in ring; join with slip st to first dc: 12 dc.

Rnd 2: Ch 1, work V-St in same st as joining and in each dc around; join with slip st to first sc: 12 V-Sts.

Rnd 3: Slip st in first V-St (ch-1 sp), ch 1, work V-St in same sp, work 2 V-Sts in next V-St, ★ work V-St in next V-St, work 2 V-Sts in next V-St; repeat from ★ around; join with slip st to first sc: 18 V-Sts.

7

Rnd 4: Slip st in first V-St, ch 1, work V-St in same sp and in next 4 V-Sts, work 2 V-Sts in next V-St, ★ work V-St in next 5 V-Sts, work 2 V-Sts in next V-St; repeat from ★ once **more**; join with slip st to first sc: 21 V-Sts.

Rnd 5: Slip st in first V-St, ch 1, work V-St in same sp and in next 5 V-Sts, work 2 V-Sts in next V-St, ★ work V-St in next 6 V-Sts, work 2 V-Sts in next V-St; repeat from ★ once **more**; join with slip st to first sc: 24 V-Sts.

Rnd 6: Slip st in first V-St, ch 1, work V-St in same sp and in next 6 V-Sts, work 2 V-Sts in next V-St, ★ work V-St in next 7 V-Sts, work 2 V-Sts in next V-St; repeat from ★ once **more**; 🎥 join with slip st to first sc changing to Black *(Fig. 3, page 46)*, cut Grey: 27 V-Sts.

Rnd 7: Slip st in first V-St, ch 1, work V-St in same sp and in next 7 V-Sts, work 2 V-Sts in next V-St, ★ work V-St in next 8 V-Sts, work 2 V-Sts in next V-St; repeat from ★ once **more**; join with slip st to first sc: 30 V-Sts.

Size Small ONLY

Rnd 8: Slip st in first V-St, ch 1, work V-St in same sp and in next 8 V-Sts, work 2 V-Sts in next V-St, ★ work V-St in next 9 V-Sts, work 2 V-Sts in next V-St; repeat from ★ once **more**; join with slip st to first sc: 33 V-Sts.

Size Medium ONLY

Rnd 8: Slip st in first V-St, ch 1, work V-St in same sp and in next 4 V-Sts, work 2 V-Sts in next V-St, ★ work V-St in next 5 V-Sts, work 2 V-Sts in next V-St; repeat from ★ around; join with slip st to first sc: 35 V-Sts.

Size Large ONLY

Rnd 8: Slip st in first V-St, ch 1, work V-St in same sp and in next 2 V-Sts, work 2 V-Sts in next V-St, ★ work V-St in next 4 V-Sts, work 2 V-Sts in next V-St, (work V-St in next 3 V-Sts, work 2 V-Sts in next V-St) twice; repeat from ★ once **more**; join with slip st to first sc: 37 V-Sts.

All Sizes

Rnds 9-11: Slip st in first V-St, ch 1, work V-St in same sp and in each V-St around; join with slip st to first sc.

Rnd 12: Slip st in first V-St, ch 1, work V-St in same sp and in each V-St around; join with slip st to first sc changing to Grey, cut Black.

Rnds 13-18: Slip st in first V-St, ch 1, work V-St in same sp and in each V-St around; join with slip st to first sc.

Rnd 19: Slip st in first V-St, ch 1, work V-St in same sp and in each V-St around; join with slip st to first sc changing to Black, cut Grey.

Rnds 20-22: Slip st in first V-St, ch 1, work V-St in same sp and in each V-St around; join with slip st to first sc, do **not** finish off.

Band

Rnd 1: Ch 1, sc in same st as joining, skip next ch-1 sp, (sc in next 2 sts, skip next ch-1 sp) around to last dc, sc in last dc; join with slip st to first sc: 66{70-74} sc.

Rnds 2-7: Ch 1, sc in same st as joining and in each sc around; join with slip st to first sc.

Finish off.

POP STAR

⬤■◻◻ **EASY +**

SIZE INFORMATION

Size: Small {Medium-Large}

Fits Head Circumference: 19{21-23}"/48.5{53.5-58.5} cm

SHOPPING LIST

Yarn (Medium Weight)

[5 ounces, 256 yards
(141 grams, 234 meters)
per skein]:

☐ 1 skein

Crochet Hook

☐ Size I (5.5 mm)

or size needed for gauge

Additional Supplies

☐ Yarn needle

Size Note: We have printed the instructions for the sizes in different colors to make it easier for you to find:

• Size Small in Blue

• Size Medium in Pink

• Size Large in Green

Instructions in Black apply to all sizes.

GAUGE INFORMATION

In Body pattern,

(Cluster, ch 1) 8 times and

7 rnds = 4" (10 cm)

In Band pattern,

7 ridges (14 rows) = 4" (10 cm)

Gauge Swatch: 3½" (9 cm) diameter

Work same as Body, page 14, through Rnd 2: 16 Clusters and 16 ch-2 sps.

──STITCH GUIDE──

 **BEGINNING CLUSTER**

(uses one sp)

Ch 3, ★ YO, insert hook in sp indicated, YO and pull up a loop, YO and draw through 2 loops on hook; repeat from ★ once **more**, YO and draw through all 3 loops on hook.

CLUSTER (uses one sp)

★ YO, insert hook in sp indicated, YO and pull up a loop, YO and draw through 2 loops on hook; repeat from ★ 2 times **more**, YO and draw through all 4 loops on hook.

INSTRUCTIONS
Body

Ch 6; join with slip st to form a ring.

Rnd 1 (Right side)**:** Work Beginning Cluster in ring, ch 3, (work Cluster in ring, ch 3) 7 times; join with slip st to top of Beginning Cluster: 8 Clusters and 8 ch-3 sps.

Note: Loop a short piece of yarn around any stitch to mark Rnd 1 as **right** side.

Rnd 2: Slip st in first ch-3 sp, work (Beginning Cluster, ch 2, Cluster, ch 2) in same sp, (work Cluster, ch 2) twice in next ch-3 sp and in each ch-3 sp around; join with slip st to top of Beginning Cluster: 16 Clusters and 16 ch-2 sps.

Rnd 3: Slip st in first ch-2 sp, work (Beginning Cluster, ch 1, Cluster, ch 1) in same sp, (work Cluster, ch 1) twice in each of next 2 ch-2 sps, work Cluster in next ch-2 sp, ch 1, ★ (work Cluster, ch 1) twice in each of next 3 ch-2 sps, work Cluster in next ch-2 sp, ch 1; repeat from ★ around; join with slip st to top of Beginning Cluster: 28 Clusters and 28 ch-1 sps.

Rnd 4: Slip st in first ch-1 sp, work Beginning Cluster in same sp, ch 1, (work Cluster in next ch-1 sp, ch 1) twice, (work Cluster, ch 1) twice in next ch-1 sp, ★ (work Cluster in next ch-1 sp, ch 1) 3 times, (work Cluster, ch 1) twice in next ch-1 sp; repeat from ★ around; join with slip st to top of Beginning Cluster: 35 Clusters and 35 ch-1 sps.

Rnd 5: Slip st in first ch-1 sp, work Beginning Cluster in same sp, ch 1, (work Cluster in next ch-1 sp, ch 1) 5 times, (work Cluster, ch 1) twice in next ch-1 sp, ★ (work Cluster in next ch-1 sp, ch 1) 6 times, (work Cluster, ch 1) twice in next ch-1 sp; repeat from ★ around; join with slip st to top of Beginning Cluster: 40 Clusters and 40 ch-1 sps.

Size Small ONLY

Rnd 6: Slip st in first ch-1 sp, work Beginning Cluster in same sp, ch 1, (work Cluster in next ch-1 sp, ch 1) 8 times, (work Cluster, ch 1) twice in next ch-1 sp, ★ (work Cluster in next ch-1 sp, ch 1) 14 times, (work Cluster, ch 1) twice in next ch-1 sp; repeat from ★ once **more**; join with slip st to top of Beginning Cluster: 43 Clusters and 43 ch-1 sps.

Size Medium ONLY

Rnd 6: Slip st in first ch-1 sp, work Beginning Cluster in same sp, ch 1, (work Cluster in next ch-1 sp, ch 1) 6 times, (work Cluster, ch 1) twice in next ch-1 sp, ★ (work Cluster in next ch-1 sp, ch 1) 7 times, (work Cluster, ch 1) twice in next ch-1 sp; repeat from ★ around; join with slip st to top of Beginning Cluster: 45 Clusters and 45 ch-1 sps.

Size Large ONLY

Rnd 6: Slip st in first ch-1 sp, work Beginning Cluster in same sp, ch 1, (work Cluster in next ch-1 sp, ch 1) twice, (work Cluster, ch 1) twice in next ch-1 sp, ★ (work Cluster in next ch-1 sp, ch 1) 5 times, (work Cluster, ch 1) twice in next ch-1 sp; repeat from ★ around; join with slip st to top of Beginning Cluster: 47 Clusters and 47 ch-1 sps.

All Sizes

Rnd 7: Slip st in first ch-1 sp, work Beginning Cluster in same sp, ch 1, (work Cluster in next ch-1 sp, ch 1) around; join with slip st to top of Beginning Cluster.

Repeat Rnd 7 until Body measures approximately 7½{8-8½}"/ 19{20.5-21.5} cm from beginning ring.

Next Rnd: Slip st in first ch-1 sp, ch 1, sc in same sp, (2 sc in next ch-1 sp, sc in next ch-1 sp) around; join with slip st to first sc: 64{67-70} sc.

Last Rnd: Ch 1, sc in same st as joining and in each sc around; join with slip st to first sc, finish off.

Band

Ch 10.

Row 1 (Right side)**:** Sc in second ch from hook and in each ch across: 9 sc.

Note: Mark Row 1 as **right** side.

Row 2: Turn; sc in 🎥 Back Loop Only of each sc across *(Fig. 1, page 45)*.

Repeat Row 2 for pattern until Band measures approximately 19{21-23}"/48.5{53.5-58.5} cm when slightly stretched, ending by working a **wrong** side row.

Finish off, leaving a long end for sewing.

Thread yarn needle with long end. 🎥 Whipstitch last row of Band to beginning ch *(Fig. 4, page 46)*, then whipstitch Band to Last Rnd of Body using same end.

BLOSSOM

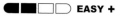 **EASY +**

SIZE INFORMATION

Size: Small {Medium-Large}

Fits Head Circumference: 18{20-22}"/45.5{51-56} cm

Size Note: We have printed the instructions for the sizes in different colors to make it easier for you to find:

• Size Small in Blue

• Size Medium in Pink

• Size Large in Green

Instructions in Black apply to all sizes.

GAUGE INFORMATION

With larger size hook, in pattern,

   10 tr = 4" (10 cm)

Gauge Swatch: 3¾" (9.5 cm)

Work same as Body through Rnd 2:
24 dc.

──STITCH GUIDE──

■◄ TREBLE CROCHET

   (abbreviated tr)

YO twice, insert hook in st or sp indicated, YO and pull up a loop (4 loops on hook), (YO and draw through 2 loops on hook) 3 times.

INSTRUCTIONS
Body

With larger size hook, ch 5; join with slip st to form a ring.

Rnd 1 (Right side)**:** Ch 3 (**counts as first dc, now and throughout**), 11 dc in ring; join with slip st to first dc: 12 dc.

Note: Loop a short piece of yarn around any stitch to mark Rnd 1 as **right** side.

Rnd 2: Ch 3, dc in same st, 2 dc in next dc and in each dc around; join with slip st to first dc: 24 dc.

Rnd 3: Ch 4 (**counts as first tr, now and throughout**), tr in same st and in next dc, (2 tr in next dc, tr in next dc) around; join with slip st to first tr: 36 tr.

Rnd 4: Ch 1, sc in same st as joining, ch 3, skip next tr, ★ sc in next tr, ch 3, skip next tr; repeat from ★ around; join with slip st to first sc: 18 sc and 18 ch-3 sps.

Rnd 5: Slip st in first ch-3 sp, ch 1, sc in same sp, ch 3, (sc in next ch-3 sp, ch 3) around; join with slip st to first sc.

Rnd 6: Slip st in first ch-3 sp, ch 4, 2 tr in same sp, 3 tr in next ch-3 sp, (2 tr in next ch-3 sp, 3 tr in next ch-3 sp) around; join with slip st to first tr: 46 tr.

Rnds 7 and 8: Repeat Rnds 4 and 5: 23 sc and 23 ch-3 sps.

Size Small ONLY

Rnd 9: Slip st in first ch-3 sp, ch 4, tr in same sp, 2 tr in next ch-3 sp and in each ch-3 sp around; join with slip st to first tr: 46 tr.

Size Medium ONLY

Rnd 9: Slip st in first ch-3 sp, ch 4, tr in same sp, 2 tr in each of next 3 ch-3 sps, 3 tr in next ch-3 sp, ★ 2 tr in each of next 5 ch-3 sps, 3 tr in next ch-3 sp; repeat from ★ 2 times **more**; join with slip st to first tr: 50 tr.

Size Large ONLY

Rnd 9: Slip st in first ch-3 sp, ch 4, tr in same sp, 3 tr in next ch-3 sp, ★ 2 tr in each of next 2 ch-3 sps, 3 tr in next ch-3 sp; repeat from ★ around; join with slip st to first tr: 54 tr.

All Sizes

Rnd 10: Ch 1, sc in same st as joining, ch 3, skip next tr, ★ sc in next tr, ch 3, skip next tr; repeat from ★ around; join with slip st to first sc: 23{25-27} sc and 23{25-27} ch-3 sps.

Rnds 11-14: Slip st in first ch-3 sp, ch 1, sc in same sp, ch 3, (sc in next ch-3 sp, ch 3) around; join with slip st to first sc.

Change to smaller size hook.

Rnd 15: Slip st in first ch-3 sp, ch 4, tr in same sp, 2 tr in next ch-3 sp and in each ch-3 sp around; join with slip st to first tr: 46{50-54} tr.

Rnds 16 and 17: Ch 1, sc in same st as joining and in each st around; join with slip st to first sc.

Finish off.

Flower

With larger size hook and leaving a long end for sewing, ch 5; join with slip st to form a ring.

Rnd 1 (Right side)**:** Ch 3, dc in ring, ch 4, (2 dc in ring, ch 4) twice; join with slip st to first dc: 6 dc and 3 ch-4 sps.

Note: Mark Rnd 1 as **right** side.

Rnd 2: Slip st in next dc, (slip st, ch 2, 5 tr, ch 2, slip st) in next ch-4 sp and in each ch-4 sp around; join with slip st to first slip st: 3 petals.

Rnd 3: Ch 1, **turn;** ★ working in **front** of petals, slip st from **front** to **back** around post of next dc on Rnd 1 *(Fig. 2, page 46)*, ch 5; repeat from ★ around; join with slip st to first slip st: 6 ch-5 sps.

Rnd 4: Turn; (slip st, ch 2, 5 tr, ch 2, slip st) in next ch-5 sp and in each ch-5 sp around; join with slip st to first slip st, finish off.

Thread yarn needle with long beginning end. Using photo as a guide for placement, sew **wrong** side of Flower to **right** side of Body.

CAMO

◖◻◻◗ EASY +

SIZE INFORMATION

Size: Small {Medium-Large}

Fits Head Circumference: 19{21-23}"/48.5{53.5-58.5} cm

SHOPPING LIST

Yarn (Medium Weight) 🧶 MEDIUM 4

[5 ounces, 244 yards
(141 grams, 223 meters)
per skein]:

☐ 1 skein

Crochet Hook

☐ Size H (5 mm)

   or size needed for gauge

Size Note: We have printed the
instructions for the sizes in different
colors to make it easier for you to
find:

• Size Small in Blue
• Size Medium in Pink
• Size Large in Green

Instructions in Black apply to all
sizes.

GAUGE INFORMATION

In pattern,

   16 sts and 7 rnds = 4" (10 cm)

Gauge Swatch: 3½" (9 cm) diameter
Work same as Body through Rnd 3:
36 dc.

INSTRUCTIONS
Body

Ch 4; join with slip st to form a ring.

Rnd 1 (Right side)**:** Ch 1, (sc, hdc,
10 dc) in ring; do **not** join, 🎥 place
marker to mark the beginning of the
rnd *(see Markers, page 45)*: 12 sts.

Work in 🎥 Back Loops Only
throughout *(Fig. 1, page 45)*.

Rnd 2: 2 Dc in each st around: 24 dc.

Rnd 3: (Dc in next dc, 2 dc in next
dc) around: 36 dc.

Rnd 4: (Dc in next 2 dc, 2 dc in next
dc) around: 48 dc.

Rnd 5: (Dc in next 3 dc, 2 dc in next dc) around: 60 dc.

Rnd 6: (Dc in next 4 dc, 2 dc in next dc) around: 72 dc.

Size Small ONLY

Rnd 7: Dc in in each dc around.

Repeat Rnd 7 until Body measures approximately 10" (25.5 cm) from beginning ring.

Next Rnd: Dc in next 68 dc, hdc in next 2 dc, sc in next 2 dc.

Last Rnd: Sc in each st around; slip st in next sc, finish off.

Size Medium ONLY

Rnd 7: (Dc in next 5 dc, 2 dc in next dc) around: 84 dc.

Rnd 8: Dc in each dc around.

Repeat Rnd 8 until Body measures approximately 10½" (26.5 cm) from beginning ring.

Next Rnd: Dc in next 80 dc, hdc in next 2 dc, sc in next 2 dc.

Last Rnd: Sc in each st around; slip st in next sc, finish off.

Size Large ONLY

Rnd 7: (Dc in next 5 dc, 2 dc in next dc) around: 84 dc.

Rnd 8: ★ Dc in next 10 dc, 2 dc in next dc, dc in next 9 dc, 2 dc in next dc; repeat from ★ around: 92 dc.

Rnd 9: Dc in each dc around.

Repeat Rnd 9 until Body measures approximately 11" (28 cm) from beginning ring.

Next Rnd: Dc in next 88 dc, hdc in next 2 dc, sc in next 2 dc.

Last Rnd: Sc in each st around; slip st in next sc, finish off.

CLUSTERS

■■■□ **INTERMEDIATE**

SIZE INFORMATION

Size: Small {Medium-Large}

Fits Head Circumference: 19½{21-22½}"/49.5{53.5-57} cm

SHOPPING LIST

Yarn (Medium Weight)
[7 ounces, 370 yards
(198 grams, 338 meters)
per skein]:
- ☐ Grey - 1 skein
- ☐ Red - 1 skein

Crochet Hook
- ☐ Size I (5.5 mm)
  or size needed for gauge

Additional Supplies
- ☐ Yarn needle

Size Note: We have printed the instructions for the sizes in different colors to make it easier for you to find:
- Size Small in Blue
- Size Medium in Pink
- Size Large in Green

Instructions in Black apply to all sizes.

GAUGE INFORMATION

In Body pattern,
    12 sts and 8 rnds = 4" (10 cm)
In Band pattern,
    7 ridges (14 rows) = 4" (10 cm)

Gauge Swatch: 3½" (9 cm) diameter
Work same as Body through Rnd 3:
28 sc.

——STITCH GUIDE——

 CLUSTER (uses one dc)

YO, insert hook from **front** to **back** around post of dc just made *(Fig. 2, page 46)*, YO and pull up a loop (3 loops on hook), ★ YO, insert hook from **front** to **back** around same dc, YO and pull up a loop; repeat from ★ once **more** (7 loops on hook), YO and draw through 6 loops on hook, YO and draw through 2 loops on hook.

INSTRUCTIONS
Body

With Grey, ch 5; join with slip st to form a ring.

Rnd 1 (Right side): Ch 1, 14 sc in ring; join with slip st to first sc.

Note: Loop a short piece of yarn around any stitch to mark Rnd 1 as **right** side.

Rnd 2: Ch 3 (**counts as first dc, now and throughout**), dc in next sc, work Cluster, (dc in next 2 sc, work Cluster) around; join with slip st to first dc: 21 sts.

Rnd 3: Ch 1, 2 sc in same st as joining, sc in next dc and in next Cluster, ★ 2 sc in next dc, sc in next dc and in next Cluster; repeat from ★ around, join with slip st to first sc: 28 sc.

Rnd 4: Ch 3, dc in next sc, work Cluster, (dc in next 2 sc, work Cluster) around; join with slip st to first dc: 42 sts.

Rnd 5: Repeat Rnd 3: 56 sc.

Rnd 6: Ch 3, dc in next sc, work Cluster, skip next sc, ★ (dc in next 2 sc, work Cluster) twice, skip next sc; repeat from ★ 9 times **more**, dc in next 2 sc, work Cluster, skip last sc; join with slip st to first dc: 66 sts.

Rnd 7: Ch 1, sc in same st as joining, sc in next dc and in next Cluster, ★ 2 sc in next dc, sc in next dc and in next Cluster; repeat from ★ around; join with slip st to first sc: 87 sc.

Rnd 8: Ch 3, dc in next sc, work Cluster, skip next sc, ★ dc in next 2 sc, work Cluster, skip next sc; repeat from ★ around; join with slip st to first dc.

Rnds 9-20: Repeat Rnds 7 and 8, 6 times.

Rnd 21: Ch 1, sc in same st as joining, ★ skip next st, sc in next 5 sts; repeat from ★ around to last 2 sts, skip next dc, sc in last Cluster; join with slip st to first sc: 72 sc.

Rnd 22: Ch 1, sc in same st as joining and in each sc around; join with slip st to first sc, finish off.

Band

With Red, ch 8.

Row 1 (Right side)**:** Sc in second ch from hook and in each ch across: 7 sc.

Note: Mark Row 1 as **right** side.

Row 2: Turn; sc in  Back Loop Only of each sc across *(Fig. 1, page 45)*.

Repeat Row 2 for pattern until Band measures approximately 19½{21-22½}"/49.5{53.5-57} cm when slightly stretched, ending by working a **wrong** side row.

Finish off, leaving a long end for sewing.

Thread yarn needle with long end. Whipstitch last row of Band to beginning ch *(Fig. 4, page 46)*, then whipstitch Band to Rnd 22 of Body using same end.

KID STUFF-BUBBLEGUM

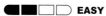 **EASY**

SIZE INFORMATION

Size: Small {Medium-Large}

Fits Head Circumference: 14{16-18}"/35.5{40.5-45.5} cm

SHOPPING LIST

Yarn (Super Bulky Weight)
[4 ounces, 64 yards
(113 grams, 59 meters) per skein]:
- ☐ 2 skeins

Crochet Hooks

- ☐ Size K (6.5 mm) **and**
- ☐ Size M/N (10 mm)
  or sizes needed for gauge

Size Note: We have printed the instructions for the sizes in different colors to make it easier for you to find:
- Size Small in Blue
- Size Medium in Pink
- Size Large in Green

Instructions in Black apply to all sizes.

GAUGE INFORMATION

With larger size hook, in pattern,
(Cluster, ch 1) 4 times and
4 rnds = 4" (10 cm)

Gauge Swatch:
2½" (6.25 cm) diameter
Work same as Body, page 34,
through Rnd 1: 12 dc.

───── STITCH GUIDE ─────

📹 **BEGINNING CLUSTER**
(uses one st or sp)

Ch 3, dc in st or sp indicated.

📹 **CLUSTER** (uses one st or sp)

★ YO, insert hook in st or sp indicated, YO and pull up a loop, YO and draw through 2 loops on hook; repeat from ★ once **more**, YO and draw through all 3 loops on hook.

INSTRUCTIONS
Body

With larger size hook, ch 5; join with slip st to form a ring.

Rnd 1 (Right side)**:** Ch 3 **(counts as first dc, now and throughout)**, 11 dc in ring; join with slip st to first dc: 12 dc.

Rnd 2: Work Beginning Cluster in same st as joining, ch 1, work Cluster in next dc, ch 1, (work Cluster, ch 1) twice in next dc, ★ (work Cluster in next dc, ch 1) twice, (work Cluster, ch 1) twice in next dc; repeat from ★ 2 times **more**; join with slip st to top of Beginning Cluster: 16 Clusters and 16 ch-1 sps.

Rnd 3: Slip st in first ch-1 sp, work Beginning Cluster in same sp, ch 1, (work Cluster in next ch-1 sp, ch 1) twice, (work Cluster, ch 1) twice in next ch-1 sp, ★ (work Cluster in next ch-1 sp, ch 1) 3 times, (work Cluster, ch 1) twice in next ch-1 sp; repeat from ★ 2 times **more**; join with slip st to top of Beginning Cluster: 20 Clusters and 20 ch-1 sps.

Rnds 4-8: Slip st in first ch-1 sp, work Beginning Cluster in same sp, ch 1, (work Cluster in next ch-1 sp, ch 1) around; join with slip st to top of Beginning Cluster.

Band

Change to smaller size hook.

Size Small ONLY

Rnd 1: Ch 1, sc in first ch-1 sp, 2 sc in next ch-1 sp, (sc in next ch-1 sp, 2 sc in next ch-1 sp) around; join with slip st to first sc: 30 sc.

Rnds 2-4: Ch 1, sc in same st as joining and in each sc around; join with slip st to first sc.

Finish off.

Size Medium ONLY

Rnd 1: Ch 1, 2 sc in each of first 2 ch-1 sps, ★ sc in next ch-1 sp, 2 sc in each of next 2 ch-1 sps; repeat from ★ around; join with slip st to first sc: 34 sc.

Rnds 2-4: Ch 1, sc in same st as joining and in each sc around; join with slip st to first sc.

Finish off.

Size Large Only

Rnd 1: Ch 1, ★ 2 sc in each of next 9 ch-1 sps, sc in next ch-1 sp; repeat from ★ once **more**; join with slip st to first sc: 38 sc.

Rnds 2-4: Ch 1, sc in same st as joining and in each sc around; join with slip st to first sc.

Finish off.

■■□□□ **EASY**

SIZE INFORMATION

Size: Small {Medium-Large}

Fits Head Circumference: 14{16-18}"/35.5{40.5-45.5} cm

SHOPPING LIST

Yarn (Medium Weight)

[5 ounces, 244 yards
(141 grams, 223 meters)
per skein]:
- ☐ 1 skein

Crochet Hook
- ☐ Size H (5 mm)

  or size needed for gauge

Additional Supplies
- ☐ Yarn needle
- ☐ Sewing needle
- ☐ Matching thread
- ☐ Button - ¾" (19 mm)

Size Note: We have printed the instructions for the sizes in different colors to make it easier for you to find:

- Size Small in Blue
- Size Medium in Pink
- Size Large in Green

Instructions in Black apply to all sizes.

GAUGE INFORMATION

In pattern,

15 sts and 7 dc rows = 4" (10 cm)

Gauge Swatch:

2½" (6.25 cm) diameter

Work same as Body, page 38, through Rnd 3: 30 sc.

STITCH GUIDE

SINGLE CROCHET 2 TOGETHER
(abbreviated sc2tog)

Pull up a loop in each of next 2 dc, YO and draw through all 3 loops on hook **(counts as one sc).**

INSTRUCTIONS
Body

Ch 5; join with slip st to form a ring.

Rnd 1 (Right side)**:** Ch 1, 10 sc in ring; do **not** join, 📹 place marker to mark beginning of rnd *(see Markers, page 45)*: 10 sc.

Note: Loop a short piece of yarn around any stitch to mark Rnd 1 as **right** side.

Work in 📹 Back Loops Only throughout *(Fig. 1, page 45)*.

Rnd 2: 2 Dc in each sc around: 20 dc.

Rnd 3: (Sc in next dc, 2 sc in next dc) around: 30 sc.

Rnd 4: (Dc in next 2 sc, 2 dc in next sc) around: 40 dc.

Rnd 5: (2 Sc in next dc, sc in next 3 dc) around: 50 sc.

Rnd 6: (Dc in next 4 sc, 2 dc in next sc) around: 60 dc.

Rnd 7: (Sc in next 4 dc, 2 sc in next dc) around: 72 sc.

Rnd 8: Dc in each sc around.

Sizes Small & Medium ONLY
Rnd 9: Sc in each dc around.

Size Large ONLY
Rnd 9: (Sc in next 5 sc, 2 sc in next sc) around: 84 sc.
All Sizes
Rnd 10: Dc in each sc around.

Rnd 11: Sc in each dc around.

Rnds 12 thru 16{17-18}: Dc in each st around.

Band
Size Small ONLY
Rnd 1: (Sc in next 2 dc, sc2tog) around: 54 sc.

Sizes Medium & Large ONLY
Rnd 1: (Sc in next 4 dc, sc2tog) around: {60-70} sc.

All Sizes

Rnds 2-4: Sc in each sc around.

Rnd 5: Sc in each sc around; slip st in next sc, finish off.

Flower

Leaving a long end for sewing, ch 5; join with slip st to form a ring.

Rnd 1 (Right side)**:** Ch 5, (dc, ch 2) 5 times in ring; join with slip st to third ch of beginning ch-5: 6 ch-2 sps.

Note: Mark Rnd 1 as **right** side.

Rnd 2: (Slip st, ch 2, 3 dc, ch 2, slip st) in first ch-2 sp and in each ch-2 sp around; join with slip st to first slip st, finish off.

Using sewing needle and matching thread, sew Button to **right** side of Flower center. Thread yarn needle with long beginning end and sew **wrong** side of Flower to **right** side of Body.

SIZE INFORMATION

Size: Small {Medium-Large}

Fits Head Circumference: 14{16-18}"/35.5{40.5-45.5} cm

Yarn (Super Bulky Weight) 🧶 6 SUPER BULKY

[6 ounces, 106 yards
(170 grams, 97 meters) per skein]:

☐ Cream - 1 skein

☐ Brown - 1 skein

Crochet Hook

☐ Size N/P (10 mm)

or size needed for gauge

Size Note: We have printed the instructions for the sizes in different colors to make it easier for you to find:

Size Small in Blue

Size Medium in Pink

Size Large in Green

Instructions in Black apply to all sizes.

GAUGE INFORMATION

8 hdc and 6 rnds = 4"(10 cm)

Gauge Swatch: 4" (10 cm) diameter
Work same as Body through Rnd 2:
20 hdc.

———STITCH GUIDE———

📹 **SINGLE CROCHET 2 TOGETHER**
(abbreviated sc2tog)

Pull up a loop in each of next 2 hdc,
YO and draw through all 3 loops on
hook **(counts as one sc)**.

INSTRUCTIONS
Body

With Cream, ch 5; join with slip st to
form a ring.

Rnd 1 (Right side)**:** Ch 3 **(counts as
first dc)**, 9 dc in ring; join with slip st
to first dc: 10 dc.

Rnd 2: Ch 2 **(counts as first hdc,
now and throughout)**, hdc in same
st as joining, 2 hdc in next dc and in
each dc around; join with slip st to
first hdc: 20 hdc.

Rnd 3: Ch 2, 2 hdc in next hdc, (hdc in next hdc, 2 hdc in next hdc) around; join with slip st to first hdc: 30 hdc.

Rnd 4: Ch 2, hdc in next hdc, 2 hdc in next hdc, (hdc in next 2 hdc, 2 hdc in next hdc) around; join with slip st to first hdc: 40 hdc.

Rnds 5-7: Ch 2, hdc in next hdc and in each hdc around; join with slip st to first hdc.

Rnd 8: Ch 2, hdc in next hdc and in each hdc around; 🎥 join with slip st to first hdc changing to Brown *(Fig. 3, page 46)*, cut Cream.

Rnds 9 thru 11{12-13}: Ch 2, hdc in next hdc and in each hdc around; join with slip st to first hdc.

Band
Size Small ONLY
Rnd 1: Ch 1, sc in same st as joining and in next hdc, sc2tog, (sc in next 2 hdc, sc2tog) around; join with slip st to first sc: 30 sc.

Rnds 2-4: Ch 1, sc in each sc around join with slip st to first sc.

Finish off.

Size Medium ONLY
Rnd 1: Ch 1, sc in same st as joining and in next 3 hdc, (sc2tog, sc in next 4 hdc) around; join with slip st to first sc: 34 sc.

Rnds 2-4: Ch 1, sc in each sc around join with slip st to first sc.

Finish off.

Size Large ONLY
Rnd 1: Ch 1, sc in same st as joining and in next 17 hdc, sc2tog, sc in next 18 hdc, sc2tog; join with slip st to first sc: 38 sc.

Rnds 2-4: Ch 1, sc in each sc around join with slip st to first sc.

Finish off.

GENERAL INSTRUCTIONS

ABBREVIATIONS

ch(s)	chain(s)
cm	centimeters
dc	double crochet(s)
hdc	half double crochet(s)
mm	millimeters
Rnd(s)	Round(s)
sc	single crochet(s)
sc2tog	single crochet 2 together
sp(s)	space(s)
st(s)	stitch(es)
tr	treble crochet(s)
YO	yarn over

SYMBOLS & TERMS

★ — work instructions following ★ as many **more** times as indicated in addition to the first time.

( ) or **[ ]** — work enclosed instructions **as many** times as specified by the number immediately following **or work** all enclosed instructions in the stitch or space indicated **or** contains explanatory remarks.

colon (:) — the number(s) given after a colon at the end of a row or round denote(s) the number of stitches or spaces you should have on that row or round.

CROCHET TERMINOLOGY		
UNITED STATES		**INTERNATIONAL**
slip stitch (slip st)	=	single crochet (sc)
single crochet (sc)	=	double crochet (dc)
half double crochet (hdc)	=	half treble crochet (htr)
double crochet (dc)	=	treble crochet(tr)
treble crochet (tr)	=	double treble crochet (dtr)
double treble crochet (dtr)	=	triple treble crochet (ttr)
triple treble crochet (tr tr)	=	quadruple treble crochet (qtr)
skip	=	miss

CROCHET HOOKS															
U.S.	B-1	C-2	D-3	E-4	F-5	G-6	H-8	I-9	J-10	K-10½	L-11	M/N-13	N/P-15	P/Q	Q	S
Metric - mm	2.25	2.75	3.25	3.5	3.75	4	5	5.5	6	6.5	8	9	10	15	16	19

■□□□	**BEGINNER**	Projects for first-time crocheters using basic stitches. Minimal shaping.
■■□□	**EASY**	Projects using yarn with basic stitches, repetitive stitch patterns, simple color changes, and simple shaping and finishing.
■■■□	**INTERMEDIATE**	Projects using a variety of techniques, such as basic lace patterns or color patterns, mid-level shaping and finishing.
■■■■	**EXPERIENCED**	Projects with intricate stitch patterns, techniques and dimension, such as non-repeating patterns, multi-color techniques, fine threads, small hooks, detailed shaping and refined finishing.

GAUGE

xact gauge is **essential** for proper ze. Before beginning your project, ake the sample swatch given the individual instructions in e yarn and hook specified. After ompleting the swatch, measure counting your stitches and rows arefully. If your swatch is larger smaller than specified, **make nother, changing hook size to get e correct gauge**. Keep trying until ou find the size hook that will give ou the specified gauge.

MARKERS

Markers are used to help distinguish the beginning of each round being worked. Place a 2" (5 cm) scrap piece of yarn before the first stitch of each round, moving marker after each round is complete.

BACK LOOP ONLY

Work only in loop(s) indicated by arrow *(Fig. 1)*.

Fig. 1

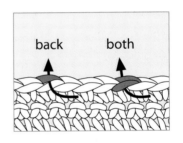

Yarn Weight Symbol & Names	LACE **0**	SUPER FINE **1**	FINE **2**	LIGHT **3**	MEDIUM **4**	BULKY **5**	SUPER BULKY **6**
Type of Yarns in Category	Fingering, 10-count crochet thread	Sock, Fingering Baby	Sport, Baby	DK, Light Worsted	Worsted, Afghan, Aran	Chunky, Craft, Rug	Bulky, Roving
Crochet Gauge* Ranges in Single Crochet to 4" (10 cm)	32-42 double crochets**	21-32 sts	16-20 sts	12-17 sts	11-14 sts	8-11 sts	5-9 sts
Advised Hook Size Range	Steel*** 6,7,8 Regular hook B-1	B-1 to E-4	E-4 to 7	7 to I-9	I-9 to K-10.5	K-10.5 to M-13	M-13 and larger

*GUIDELINES ONLY: The chart above reflects the most commonly used gauges and hook sizes for specific yarn categories.

** Lace weight yarns are usually crocheted on larger-size hooks to create lacy openwork patterns. Accordingly, a gauge range is difficult to determine. Always follow the gauge stated in your pattern.

*** Steel crochet hooks are sized differently from regular hooks–the higher the number the smaller the hook, which is the reverse of regular hook sizing.

WORKING AROUND POST OF A STITCH

Work around post of stitch indicated, inserting hook from **front** to **back** *(Fig. 2)*.

Fig. 2

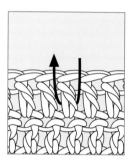

CHANGING COLORS

Insert hook in stitch indicated, drop old yarn, with new yarn *(Fig. 3)*, YO and draw through both loops on hook.

Fig. 3

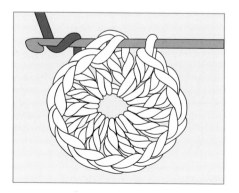

WHIPSTITCH

With **wrong** sides together, sew through both pieces once to secure the beginning of the seam, leaving an ample yarn end to weave in late Insert the needle from **front** to **bac** through **both** strands on **each** piec *(Fig. 4)*. Bring the needle around an insert it from **front** to **back** through the next strands on both pieces. Repeat along the edge, being careful to match stitches and rows.

Fig. 4

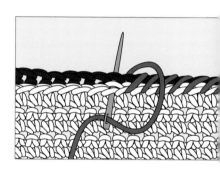

YARN INFORMATION

The Beanies in this book were made using a variety of yarn weights. Any brand of the specified weight of yarn may be used. It is best to refer to the yardage/meters when determining how many balls or skeins to purchase. Remember, to arrive at the finished size, it is the GAUGE/TENSION that is important, not the brand of yarn.

For your convenience, listed below are the specific yarns used to create our photography models.

STRIPES
Red Heart® With Love®

Navy - #1801 Navy

Blue - #1814 True Blue

ZIGZAG
Red Heart® With Love®

Grey - #1401 Pewter

Black - #1012 Black

POP STAR
Red Heart® Soft®

#4422 Tangerine

BLOSSOM
Lion Brand® Homespun®

#322 Baroque

CAMO
Red Heart® Super Saver®

#0971 Camouflage

CLUSTERS
Red Heart® With Love®

Grey - #1401 Pewter

Red - #1914 Berry Red

KID STUFF - BUBBLEGUM
Lion Brand® Hometown USA®

#208 Phoenix Azalea

KID STUFF - FLOWER CHILD
Red Heart® Super Saver®

#0972 Pink Camo

KID STUFF - GUY'S
Lion Brand® Wool-Ease® Thick & Quick®

Cream - #099 Fisherman

Brown - #404 Wood

We have made every effort to ensure that these instructions are accurate and complete. W
cannot, however, be responsible for human error, typographical mistakes, or variations i
individual work.

Production Team: Instructional/Technical Editor - Sarah J. Green;
Editorial Writer - Susan Frantz Wiles; Graphic Artist - Jessica Bramlett;
Senior Graphic Artist - Lora Puls; Photo Stylist - Lori Wenger; and
Photographers - Jason Masters and Ken West.